Behind the Series

Behind the Series
Reflections on Ethnography
Joseph C Wilson

Special Thanks

Over the last four years, I have met incredible people along my various journeys. First of all who deserve thanks are the college professors who put up with my wild antics. The next people that deserve a big thanks are all of my various friends and family members who helped support my journeys- whether it was getting my bus tickets when I had no cell or internet service in rural Wyoming, for driving down to the beach to buy me dinner in California, or even for suggesting a good place to get brunch in Hawaii.

To all the friends I made along all of these adventures, you all deserve a shout out- whether I bunked with you in a hostel, you let me crash on your couch, or you let me buy you a beer while we talked about sports. Finally- and maybe most importantly- I want to thank all the athletes I met along the way. Nicole Ross, Gwendolyn Oxenham, Amberley Snyder, Manon Brunet and Martina Criscio, Claire Bevilacqua and Savannah Bradley; and Beverley Yanez and Nahomi Kawasumi. You all helped encourage my crazy idea to document the lives of women in a wide and diverse range of sports.

Prologue

"Different" Ximena Sarinana

I like to think that everyone has at least some instinctive drive to explore the unknown. Whether that is to discover a new element on the Periodic Table, eat foods they have never tried before, or- upon seeing some great wave out on the horizon- to paddle out and try to surf. For anthropologists- especially socio-cultural anthropologists- we share the common drive to explore the everyday lives of other humans.

I realized this drive when I was five years old when my dad took my two siblings and I down to Cancun for a work trip. We stayed at a hotel on the beach, and I remember transitioning from the beach to the pool and the cool trinkets in the hotel lobby gift shop. I also remember the bus ride to Chichen Itza where we explored the remains of a Classic Era Maya metropolis. There were stone pyramids, an athletic arena, and the pillars from the original market.

Exploring this new place as a five year old inspired me to want to explore more- both places around the world and places around time. It's a major reason why I majored in history and anthropology in college. Pretty much everyone I knew in college had some kind of similar story. Maybe they went to Europe with their family as a kid, or to the Caribbean, or even on a Safari in South Africa.

All of us college students knew we needed to go and explore, but the problem was that none of us knew how- or when- or where. When I went on my first solo adventure- the first time I traveled anywhere by myself- I found out one of my favorite musicians was playing a concert in New Orleans. The Crescent City was only a hundred dollar round-trip train ride away, and I had already been to the city once before. I decided, "why the heck not?" and booked my train, bought my concert ticket, and headed to New Orleans.

I think a lot of anthropologists often leave undergraduate school either heading to graduate school or some other path with the idea that they should study something that holds value- such as studying disappearing cultures in Oceania, or digging up ancient human skeletons in the Rift Valley. These are both certainly important subjects, but the problem is no one is capable of making other people care about a topic if the writer is not passionate about it. Therefore, the first step to planning a place to travel is by asking first, "Where do I want to go?"

It seems reasonable- almost a "no brainer"- but a lot of people fall into the rut of hearing other people's stories of travel and want to simply repeat the adventure. The problem is that the real adventure is exploring one's self. The destination itself never matters- but the journey; as every cheesy travel ad likes to claim. But it's true. The adventure is exploring a path that you yourself chose to walk down- regardless of what sights, destinations, or even dangers you happen to find along the way.

The next step is to know where to stay once you get to where you've picked on the map. Hotels are an obvious choice- but are often expensive, especially for people fresh out of college or still in college. Plus, if you are traveling alone, you have almost no chance at meeting new people- which if this is an anthropological trip, meeting people is the main reason to travel. Therefore, the best two options I suggest for traveling are hostels and couchsurfing.

Hostels are amazing because they are usually set up with multiple "bunk rooms" with several beds in each room- forcing people to meet each other. There are also usually shared kitchens which force strangers to cook and eat with each other. Whether I stayed at a specific hostel for two nights or twenty, some of the best friends I have today are people I met at hostels along my travels. Hostel guests are not the only ones you should try to get to know either. People who work at hostels often have a wealth of knowledge about secret local spots worth checking out. In one hostel in Italy, one of the employees shared the haunted history of the city with me- which I never would have learned from travel books or hotels.

Couchsurfing is also an invaluable asset. Hostels in the United States are few and far between (in the actual literal sense that the few hostels that exist can sometimes have distances of hundreds of miles between them) which can make lodging expensive. The great thing about the United States is that the country has State and National Parks almost everywhere; meaning a person can drive for a day, find a camping spot for usually the price of a hostel, pitch their tent (or sleep in their car), then leave in the morning and keep driving. (And I highly suggest doing this as well.)

The other great part is that a lot of world travelers trying to save money live in the United States. There is a website called Couchsurfing where members all over the world advertise their house or apartment as a location from free lodging. Unlike AirBnB, Couchsurfer hosts typically spend time with their guests and show them unique places only locals would know about in their city or town. This is a great way to meet locals and find hidden gems in towns and cities along your travels.

My suggestion for Couchsurfing though is that while the service does not require a guest to pay their host, I usually bring either a book or some kind of gift for people who host me. It's a great way to thank your guest for letting you stay at their place, and it gives the guest a way to remember you. I also suggest staying with a specific host for no more than four nights. (Since you're staying for free, don't take advantage of the situation.)

"Keep Diggin'" Larkin Poe

Sometimes the hardest part of planning for an adventure is trying to figure out what to pack. I grew up going backpacking a lot, so I got used to packing light. When I travel- whether for a weekend or for multiple months; I only ever bring my computer bag and a single carry-on bag. I'll pack one week's worth of clothes, my laptop, and a notebook for journaling. Sometimes, I'll pack a book or two to read along the way. Finally, I bring gifts for either the hostels or Couchsurfing hosts I'm staying with.

Packing clothes can be difficult when the only space I have is a single carry-on bag. I also have to predict (or at least try to) what exactly I'm dressing for. In the event that I find a beach, pool, or hot tub; I always pack a swimsuit. If wherever I am gets cold, I'll always pack two pairs of pants. If wherever I am gets hot, I'll always pack two pairs of shorts. The great part of this is rule number 1 with clothing; jeans go with everything. Rule number two is that no one judges anyone who wears the same pair of shorts or pants two or three days in the same week. I'll pack one t-shirt for each day of the week and one button-up shirt with a tie.

Every once in a while someone invites me to some formal event where I feel the need to wear a tie. Hence the button-up shirt. If your wardrobe resembles mine in any way, your jeans will be your most formal leg-based clothing item; so find a shirt that matches your jeans. If it rains where I'm going, I always bring a rain jacket-black without any markings or designs. This is important because I can use it as a sports jacket if necessary- allowing me to pair it with my formal attire. I'll also bring a light hoodie or hooded jacket-which I can pair with the rain jacket if it gets really cold out.

Obviously a toothbrush and deodorant are necessary too, but you can buy toothpaste anywhere- as well as sunscreen; so you won't need to worry about trying to guess if your toothpaste is too big to get past security at airports. You can also always buy soap wherever you go for showering, so just worry about remembering your towel. Sometimes I will bring a small one if I know there will be no beach for me to visit; but I can roll up a full-sized beach towel and use it as a pillow if I need one. (Which happens more than you would think.)

Finally, bringing a friend is always great. I only ever traveled with another person for one of my trips- and only for a portion of the adventure- but having a second person to follow along can make a big difference. Also, it is pretty common to find people at the hostel you're staying at that might be wanting to split the cost of renting a car and heading to a local park for the weekend. These "micro trips" as I call them will happen a lot if you stay at a hostel, so having someone to split a car rental fee with (or taxi fees, etc.) can help make traveling cheaper.

"Out on the Road" Norah Jones

Preparing for an adventure also requires preliminary research. Whether you are traveling to document something specific, or just going on vacation; it's important to have some prior knowledge of the places you're going. The quick tips are to understand the laws of whatever state or country you are visiting- including if you need a travel visa to visit. (Sometimes, the list of countries requiring visas can be surprising.) It's also important to understand a few phrases of whatever the local language is. The important things like "hello" and "thank you" are especially versatile.

It's also important to have at least a rough plan for your travels. You can always deviate from the path you choose later on, but you'll never go anywhere if you don't have some kind of plan for where you might be going. A good place to start is deciding where you want to start and where you want to finish. This might be a specific city you will be flying in and out of. (You might fly into Milan, Italy for example, travel around Europe, then fly back home through Milan again- thus allowing you to start and end at the same airport.)

A good way for finding a place to start and end is by toying around with online travel agencies and looking for the cheapest airports in a given region to fly in and out of. Trains in Europe specifically are extremely affordable, so flying into Milan and taking the train to Berlin is actually cheaper than flying directly into Berlin- plus you have the opportunity to travel across the Alps.

If you are going somewhere to learn more about a specific subject (like women's sports!) you should research that topic before you go. I always looked into the top athletes in whatever sport I was studying, read up on their biographies, and found books on the topic of the sport I was studying to either read before or during my trips. If you are traveling for a specific event- like a sporting event or a music festival- make sure you get real tickets. Scalpers are always selling fake tickets, and possessing a fake ticket while trying to get into the event will often get you into more trouble than trying to sneak in without a ticket at all.

Also- especially for music festivals- pick which artists you want to see the most. These things usually have so many different bands playing throughout that it is impossible to hear every performance. Make a plan for who you want to see and know when and at what stage they are performing at. For sporting events- especially multi-game events like a World Cup or the Olympics- there will also be various different events on the same day or at the same time. Decide what you're going to see before you go and get the appropriate tickets or wristbands.

More important than any of those though- is to sometimes not plan or research. I often found myself thinking I knew everything I knew about a subject or place only to discover I was wrong. Being ignorant of a subject or a place can often make it more fun. That's part of what makes meeting new people amazing. I learned more about fencing- a sport I've been involved in since I was fifteen- from people I met in Leipzig. I learned there was so much more than what I already knew regarding my favorite sport.

When I first started my surfing study, I knew almost nothing about the sport. To make up for my knowledge deficit, I asked anyone I met about what I was seeing (in terms of competition) and reading (in terms of news and statistics). People were always happy to tell me about their favorite sport and by the time I was nearing the end of my study, people started mistaking *me* for the surfing expert. The takeaway here is to never be afraid to ask questions and to listen when someone offers to explain things about what might help you along your journey. (This is also a pro tip for Dungeons and Dragons by the way.)

"Boom Fire" HIRIE

Over the years, I have stayed at a lot of hostels- including some incredibly beautiful or incredibly unique locations. From those on the beach to those on hills; hostels have been an incredible way for me to get acquainted with both local towns and cities- and to meet some amazing world travelers. Oftentimes, even the most incredibly beautiful buildings or cleanest dorm rooms pale in comparison to the effect that an amazing board game night can have on making a hostel memorable. Trying to figure out which hostel experiences were my five favorite was its own obstacle to overcome. But after hours of deep though (and nostalgia for past travels) I tackled the topic and laid out a top five list of my favorite hostel experiences.

The fifth place spot goes to The North Shore Hostel in Maui. (So shout out to you all over there!) The North Shore Hostel Maui is located in Wailuku on the Hawaiian island of Maui. I chose this particular hostel for a few reasons. I would be in Maui for two weeks while studying the second part of my field study on the role of women in surfing. I usually look for hostels on Hostel.com (a website I suggest for anyone looking for hostels in specific towns or cities). It was the second cheapest hostel on the island and while it was far from the tournament site I needed to be going to, it was close to the airport. But none of those reasons are why North Shore Hostel Maui earned its spot on my list.

When I first arrived in Wailuku from my flights from Sitka, I arrived first at what I thought was the hostel. (In the dark, I had trouble finding the sign for the right building.) I went under a covered entrance to a parking lot and found a man there who asked if I was looking for the hostel. After I told him yes and admitted I was a little lost, he showed me the hostel.

"My name's Joe by the way," the man said. "And welcome to Maui!"

"My name is also Joe!" I replied, "Thanks for the help!"

I headed into the hostel where I found I arrived after lights out- when the hostel's quiet time was in effect (10pm to 7am). The only person in the lobby was a German woman (we'll refer to as

Berlin) who worked at the hostel. After signing in, Berlin took my photo for security purposes, took down the information from my passport, and showed me to my room. Throughout my stay, there were usually three office clerks at the hostel- one from Germany, one from Vermont, and one that I never really talked to who looked like the stereotypical male surfer from the 70's. All three looked like they were somewhere between ages twenty-five and thirty-five. There were also two cleaners- one a man who looked about mid forties and one a woman that looked about late twenties.

On my first morning in Wailuku, I woke up and found the hostel lobby filled with guests ages forty-five to seventy-five, meaning I was the youngest guest in the hostel by a few years. When a forty-something Russian man (who we'll call Moscow) offered to make me pancakes though, and an elderly German woman (we'll call Munich) offered to make me coffee; I felt like the local kid of the hostel visiting family on Thanksgiving (especially because it was Thanksgiving weekend).

I talked to the two about why I came to Maui and excited both when I talked about my travels in Europe. Moscow and I hung out a lot anytime I was at the hostel and I talked to Munich every morning since the two of us were usually the first two guests awake. Moscow checked out that Monday though and Munich on Tuesday. That Sunday though, I watched Moana on the balcony of the hostel with a woman from Montreal (about thirty- give or take two years) who had come out to practice her ukulele. Later that night, Montreal, Moscow, Munich, and I watched *10 Things I Hate About You* on the television.

On that Monday night, I met a couple from Lyon, France; but they only stayed a night, so I didn't get to know them well. Montreal checked out that morning, so I was back to having only Munich to talk to in the mornings. That night, I watched *Kill Bill* with the couple from Lyon and a few other guests in the hostel lobby along with Vermont- one of the other hostel office workers.

Later that week, a new batch of hostel guests came in more around my age, which is where the hostel experience became worth remembering. There was an Italian man about my age (maybe twenty-five) who we'll call Milan. There were two German men (we'll call Dusseldorf and Cologne). These three were constantly arguing over whether Italy or Germany made the best sports cars.

They also would constantly refer to me as the expert on surfing before asking me questions about the sport.

Then there were two men in their forties (one from St. Louis and another from Japan) who were in town for windsurfing. St. Louis would bring me a copy of the local newspaper anytime a front page photo featured one of the women in the surfing tournament. There was also a married couple in their thirties (one from Germany, one from Canada). There was a young man from France (we'll call Paris), a young woman from Scotland (we'll call Edinburgh), three women from Quebec (in their thirties), and a man from the border of Germany and Switzerland (we'll call Stuttgart). There were also two more people from Germany (a man who looked about thirty we'll call Leipzig- and an eighteen year old girl- we'll call Hamburg).

That second Friday I stayed at the hostel, all of the guests listed above under forty and I walked around Wailuku where there was a street festival going on after Vermont suggested we check it out. We then loaded up on beers at the nearby gas station and headed back to the hostel to party. I should add that when I party, it's not like when other people party. Where I went to college, there were certainly several house parties one could attend to play beer pong, do keg stands, and pass out from how drunk one might get- and admittedly, my house was often one of those. But my kind of party is people sitting around drinking beer and talking to each other- maybe playing board games or card games of some kind.

That Friday night, we were all drinking, playing card games, and getting to know each other- and like any responsible people; when quiet hour approached, we all cleaned up our mess and got quiet on time. That Saturday, I got lunch with Dusseldorf who was always cracking jokes and making finger pistols. We spent another evening with the hostel guests drinking and playing card games, this time with Vermont who busted out a giant version of the game Uno.

When quiet time approached, Vermont had a way of entering the lobby and letting us know in a quiet voice that quiet time was approaching. Dusseldorf, Cologne, Milan, and I decided we were too awake to go to bed so we headed out to one of the bars. (Unfortunately we were not able to convince Vermont to come with us.) That Sunday evening I sat in the hostel lobby with the couple from Germany/Canada, a new guest from Ireland (we'll call Dublin), and Edinburgh to watch *Sense and Sensibility* on the television. All of the women were surprised at my excitement over Jane Austin literature- to which I responded with staunch praise for the author and that there's nothing wrong about a man who like feminist Georgian Era fiction.

That Monday, I spent the day with the three women from Quebec and Stuttgart as we drove to the west side of the island, stopping for fresh coconut along the way before enjoying the beaches of Lahaina. We stopped into the local bar Spanky's in time for happy hour half-priced margaritas and burgers too. One of the women from Quebec had only begun learning English in the last month, so after her loud laughter ignited my statement that the party would get me banned from the bar- and after she told me she didn't know how to say what she wanted to tell me in English- I handed her a piece of paper and a pencil and told her to draw what she wanted to say.

The resulting image was a hilarious sketch in pictionary format detailing a stick-figure man in a Hawaiian shirt announcing that I would be banned from Hawaii in response to the stick figure woman laughing loudly. (I still have that sketch today by the way.) When we returned to the hostel, we grabbed beers along the way and partied with Edinburgh and Paris on the hostel balcony. After learning that Edinburg grew up dancing ballet- but never learning swing dancing, I put some electro-swing on my phone and started teaching the young Scottish woman how to swing dance- which summoned Vermont excited to hear swing music coming from the balcony.

The next morning, the Quebec women, Stuttgart, and I went to get brunch at the Tasty Crust- a nearby diner- before they checked out of the hostel. There, the women's laughter incited my belief that they would get me banned from the whole island. After they checked out, Vermont brought one of her friends to hang out with her at the hostel; and since I was the only guest there that afternoon, I spoke with both of them about sports. (Vermont's friend was a rock climber.)

After that weekend, the excitement died down, but on my last day in Wailuku, Dublin drove Hamburg, a new guest from Montreal (we'll call Montreal Vista), and I to Lahaina. Along the way, we stopped by a farmer's market before arriving at the beach town. The hostel had a great way of bringing guests together-regardless of age differences or language barriers. I was able to meet people traveling for surfing, snorkeling, windsurfing, and simply passing through on their journeys across the Pacific Ocean. Because of the North Shore Hostel Maui, I got to meet some amazing people, went to the beach with loud-laughing women, taught a Scottish woman how to swing dance, drank with guys from Germany and Italy, and watched Tarentino films with people from all over the world.

"Hot to the Touch" Grace Potter

The number four spot for top hostel experiences goes to my first ever hostel experience. When I was growing up, I went on a lot of road trips with either my dad or my grandma. My grandma would always rent hotel rooms for my siblings, my cousins, and I to stay at- including one that was part of a water park. My dad usually shifted between campgrounds and motels. When I first started traveling on my own (namely New Orleans and Chicago trips in college), I usually either stayed at cheap hotels, stayed with friends, or stayed with people I met through Couchsurfing.

The first time I stayed at a hostel was when I went to Vancouver for the FIFA Women's World Cup in 2015. I found a hostel just outside of the city so that I could stay away from the noise of the downtown area but still be within a reasonable distance from the tournament venue. The decision paid off. The hostel I stayed at was called the HI (abbreviated for Hosteling International) Jericho Beach.

Hosteling International is an international company that manages hostels across the world. (They even have memberships available for discounts at their hostels.) In Vancouver alone, the HI organization managed three separate hostels. The result was that anytime one hostel hosted an event, people staying at any of the HI hostels in the city were welcome to attend.

I stayed at the hostel for three weeks and went to two of the HI Vancouver hostels pub crawls. For the first one I ended up ditching with two girls from Washington, two men from Australia, a man from the US (I want to say New Jersey?), and a man from Brazil. We spent the majority of the evening drinking at one of the downtown HI hostels and getting to know each other- talking about our respective countries/states and what we studied in college.

During the second pub crawl, I ended up having some great conversations with a woman from New Zealand and a man from Ireland. But these two pub crawls were not what made my first hostel experience memorable.

I was in town for the FIFA Women's World Cup, and several guests at the hostel were in town for the same reason. First off, a retired FIFA referee had brought his grandson from New York to watch the tournament- so he gave me a lot of tips about what to look for during the games. There was also a woman from California, a woman from Spain, and a woman from France who were all in town for the tournament. On the night before the final game, the three invited me to come with them to a pregame party (which also happened to fall on the 4th of July) and turned into the biggest Independence Day party I had ever been to- and it was in a foreign country I might add.

The hostel also had a diner on its first floor, so I often strolled into the restaurant for breakfast or lunch for a cheap burger and beer and spoke to the people who worked there- including a young man in college trying to figure out what he wanted to do with his life. Throughout the three weeks I was at the hostel, I often sat in the hostel's TV room to watch films with a woman from Vancouver Island and a man from England, a hostel employee from Australia, the trio of world cup attending women, and the retired referee. There was also a photographer at the hostel in town for the tournament from Brazil who would often show me photos he took during the games. There were also trips to the nearby beach, pick-up games of soccer, and various late nights in the kitchen talking to people from all over the world.

My first hostel experience ever could not have been better. On top of that all, the hostel was incredibly clean, my roommates were great (even while they teased me during morning hangovers), and the friends I made there are ones I still talk to four years later. Plus the United States won the World Cup that year, so I felt pretty good about my three weeks in Vancouver.

"Mixer" Amber Mark

The number three spot goes to a hostel in San Clemente, California. The House of Trestles was designed for surfers, so when I arrived in California to research women in the sport of surfing, the hostel stood out among the others in the area- and the hostel did not disappoint. To start with, the hostel is managed by two brothers and their staff who are dedicated to managing a hostel for world travelers with an interest (at least in some part) in the sport of surfing.

From the wall murals to the bike and surf board rentals, the hostel ran a seriously professional service for traveling surfers. But on top of all of that, the staff's serious dedication to their jobs was paired equally with a serious dedication to making every single guest feel special during their stay. Within twenty-four hours of being at the hostel, members of the staff were already getting me connected to the local surf scene, and suggesting books to read on women in the sport.

The guests were incredible too. Within an hour of checking into the hostel, I headed to the beach with a man from the Netherlands, grabbed a slice of pizza by the pier, and returned in time for an interview with a local television news show for a segment on surfing. (It was a full day.) I also met two badass Irish women in town on their road trip across the United States who drove me down to the tournament the next morning and watched the competition with me.

I was at the hostel for two weeks- and most hostels typically have guests either short-term (two to seven nights) or long term (two to four weeks), so as a member of the latter group I connected with a lot of people who came and went. The first main group I hung out with consisted of a young man from Adelaide on his first trip to the United States who was on his way home to Australia after working as a camp counselor for the summer. The other two were a metal-smith from the Netherlands and a recreation guide from Toronto. The four of us spent three days during my trip shopping at the local Rip Curl outlets and swimming on the ocean.

Like me, there was one other person who used the hostel as an office- a programmer who could work anywhere where there was a wifi signal. (So why not the coolest hostel in California?) When there were days where I did not need to be at the beach for the competition, she was the only other guest still inside during the day, so the two of us rocked out to a lot of Britney Spears music in the hostel lobby.

During the second week, I spent time with two surf photographers- one from Brazil and one from Florida (technically

Florida and Georgia) who were both in town for the tournament and who both showed me some of the amazing photography they captured at the end of each day. The photographer from Florida was also working on a book about women's sports, so she invited me to a few exclusive events including a private art gala hosted by Kelly Slater. (Remember that button-up shirt and tie I mentioned before? This is why I pack that.)

One of the staff members at the hostel introduced me to a surfer friend of his too who helped both me and the photographer from Florida with our books. That same night, the hostel hosted a dance party where a woman painted head-to-toe in purple body paint sang cabaret and bossa nova while I danced the night away. I swing danced with some of the staff members- and impressed that surfer- before defeating a young Costa Rican man in a one-on-one dance-off.

On top of all of this, the hostel had weekly events including Tea Therapy Sessions on Wednesday evenings where a professional tea therapist would come by, throw down some soothing whale noises, and pass around samples of his tea of the week. On Thursdays, a professional acro-yoga instructor came by to treat guests to her craft. Adelaide and I partnered up for this during my first week and we were both laughing for the entire hour.

Apart from all of these amazing guests, staff, and instructors; there were several badass guests who also came through. There was a kick-boxer from Brazil who tested my knowledge of feminist movements from across the world, several Germans, a regular guest from San Diego, and a man from Atlanta who on one night went out to the beach with me and the woman from the Netherlands for a bonfire to introduce her to s'mores and campfire ghost stories.

"Abduction" Simonne Jones

The number two hostel on this list was an adventure in many ways. I am often reminded that when things don't go according to my expectations, I usually enjoy them the most. This is not an easy lesson to learn either (and I think a lot of people still struggle with this.) But the number two best hostel experience I had was one that turned from catastrophe to incredible. The second best hostel experience I ever had was the Schusterhostel in Germering, Bavaria.

My first night in Germering came after already being in Germany for almost three weeks. Germering is a small town outside of Munich where a lot of tourists go to binge on local beers. When I saw the hostel in Germering had a full bar without the chaos of being in the center of a city, I decided to give it a shot. To get to the hostel, I took the train from Leipzig to Munich, then a second train from Munich to Germering. From there, a Macedonian man picked me and a few other new guests up from the train station in a blue van- in which I jumped in the back after all the seats were taken. After checking into the hostel, I grabbed dinner at the restaurant outside and started drinking the local beers from the bar.

Over the course of the evening, several guests began socializing in the hostel's lobby- including a woman from Australia and England, two men from California, a young man from Australia, a young woman from South Africa, and a couple from Oregon. This oversized cast and I spent the evening playing beer pong and then watching the younger members of the group (ages seventeen to twenty) proceed to get completely wasted; leading to me being the designated "uncle" of the group bringing water to the intoxicated teens.

My only fellow "uncle" for the weekend was a French motorcyclist who- with me- would take turns taking care of the teenagers on their first trip to a country where the drinking age was below twenty-one. Daytime activities included less bodily-fluid inducing moments. One day, the lot of us went to a local lake to swim and sunbathe on the grass, followed by a group nap at the hostel, then a massive pizza feast. The next night, most of the group had left,; leaving Florida, the Californians, the Oregonians, the hostel employees, and myself to enjoy a night-time BBQ.

During my stay, the several guests at the hostel enjoyed drinking beer out of their shoes (wine when feeling classy), which they referred to as "shoeys" and which I refused to take part in. But, I did take comfort in the parting photo with the seventeen year-old from California taking one last shoey before leaving Germering to continue his adventure. For a weekend full of dorm roommates either peeing or vomiting all over my room, the stay at the Schusterhostel was still incredible- based entirely on the company of said vomiteers [because if there is going to be a term for "people who vomit," it may as well be a classy one].

"Too Young to Remember" Florrie

The number one best hostel experience I had during my four years of traveling between 2015 and 2018 goes to one that I never planned on going to. It is also the only hostel I have stayed at twice- because of how incredible my first experience was. This was a hostel that not only had incredible staff, but amazing guests I met during both of my stays; plus an excellent breakfast spread. The best hostel experience I had goes to the Castle Hostel in Genoa, Italy.

While working on my book about women in the sport of fencing, I planned for my flights to enter and depart from Milan- the largest city in Northern Italy. My original plan was to take a train from Milan to Paris, then from Paris to Leipzig- the only city I needed to be at for my study. After realizing during my first day in Milan however that I was closer to the Mediterranean Sea than I had ever been in my life, I decided I absolutely had to swim in its waters. I looked at the map on my phone and found the closest sea-side city to Milan and found Genoa. I also saw that Genoa had a hostel built out of a castle on a hill and decided then and there I had to sleep at that hostel.

After taking the train from Milan to Genoa, I had to climb a massive hill under extreme heat to reach the hostel. To make things even more strange and mysterious, the city of Genoa was built by pirates; so anyone traveling anywhere within the city has to walk through sketchy alleyways to get to where they are going. Along my climb to the hostel, I constantly second-guessed my own orienteering until I ended up at the gate of a castle on a hill. I immediately made friends with my roommates from Jersey (an island between Great Britain and France) as well as three girls from Finland.

On my first full day in Genoa, I went with the couple from Jersey to the nearby grocery store to buy cheap, boxed wine along with cheese and bread- and then partied it up like classy folks for the entire day. On my second full day, I went with the Finnish girls, a woman from New Zealand, two men from Toronto, a woman from New Jersey, and a woman from Vancouver to a nearby town via train called Bogliasco. There, I finally swam in the Mediterranean. I played Frisbee on the beach, got brunch at a restaurant on a cliff overlooking the sea (which was about ten Euros for two courses and a bottle of wine). I then got gelato with the group, spent more time on the beach, and made it back to the hostel in time to get more boxes of wine and kept that party going well into the night.

There is one photo someone took of all of us that day that I keep on my phone that always brings me back to that moment on the beach. Anytime I see that photo, I can't help but smile, remembering what might have been the greatest "why not" moment of my life. This is an important and perfect example of why sometimes, while traveling, a person has to remember that the journey is always more important than the destination. My destination for that trip was Leipzig, Germany- which was its own incredible moment. But that unplanned trip to Genoa was life-changing, and in the best possible way. Plus, it was a freaking castle!

Chapter 2: Top 5 Unexpected Moments

"Sunday" Anuhea

When it comes to anthropology, a lot of things can happen without room for foreshadowing. Whether it is a missed train, a mistake on a hotel reservation, or a last-minute notice; unplanned events will always happen during an adventure. I've been lucky enough to have several surprise moments that turned out to be some of the most incredible moments of my life.

While there were certainly several moments that I did not plan for, I want to focus on five moments that were not part of the overall field study. For example, watching the final of the women's world cup was the entire reason why I was in Canada, so that won't be in this list. The first moment and winner of the number five spot that is on this list however was my unplanned night swim in Maui.

On my first full day in Maui, I met up with a Couchsurfer (through their "meet-up" feature- a feature I suggest highly even for travelers not necessarily staying with a Couchsurfer host) to go on a hike into the Iao Valley. Vancouver and I walked all the way from my hostel to the trailhead- which took about two hours and was marked only with a "Do Not Enter" sign which is apparently Hawaiian for "The Trail Starts Here" according to Vancouver.

While hiking through the jungle mountain, Vancouver and I walked past several hikers who had turned back before reaching the end of the trail due to rough terrain. Vancouver and I kept pushing through however until we found a group of three mud-splattered Alaskans on the island for the winter. (We call these "winter birds" in Alaska.) Our two groups decided to merge into one super group and we agreed we would follow the trail all the way to its unknown end.

Upon reaching the top of the mountain, the valley appeared around us equipped with a double rainbow. I played the *Moana* soundtrack as we took several photos and talked about what we would do next. Along the hike back down to the trailhead, we decided to get an early dinner at a bar in Paia where we planned a trip to the beach. The five of us picked up beer from a gas station across the street from where we got dinner and headed to Baldwin beach as the sun set over the ocean.

While at the beach, the whole group debated over whether it was safe to swim in the water since sharks often come close to shore at night. One of the three Alaskans pointed at the massive waves breaking on the beach and told me, "Sharks hate waves like that!" to which I replied I'd make sure his quote would be written on his tombstone. After nervous laughs about the group, we all changed into our swimsuits and headed into the surf.

For the next two hours, we jumped, swam, and let the waves carry us to shore- sometimes forcefully against the sand- all the while enjoying the moonlit night sky and the waves crashing over us. After drinking the beers we brought, we all headed back to the Alaskans' van and played cards deep into the night while debating the possibility of sneaking into a resort hot tub. People were getting tired though, so the Van Life Trio drove Vancouver and I back to our respective hostels and the day was done.

I often have spontaneous moments when I meet Couchsurfer members while on my trips- and this is not the only one that will be on this list; but I rarely get to spend an entire day with someone I met through Couchsurfing if I did not actually stay with them as a guest. A couple days later, Vancouver and I split the cost of renting a car for five days and ended up meeting up with the Van Life Trio several more times before she left to continue her adventure throughout Hawaii.

"This Town" Kacey Musgraves

The number four spot goes to another "moments related to Couchsurfing" event. For my first two nights in Laramie, Wyoming during my rodeo study; I stayed at a local motel while trying to find a Couchsurfer host in the small town. I ended up finding a host, but since I already had the motel room for another night, my eventual host offered to take me around for the Fourth of July anyway.

In the morning, Dubai (a Laramie local soon to be leaving Wyoming for a job in the UAE) picked me up and brought me to meet up with his friends and girlfriend for *America Has a Birthday*- Laramie's annual Independence Day celebration. In downtown Laramie, we all listened to music, played several carnival games (including human foosball) and got lunch at Taco John's (the greatest fast food restaurant).

After lunch, we all headed out of town, first to a state park where snow still decked the tops of the mountains and the little lakes perfectly reflected the blue sky above. After our short venture into the wilderness, we headed to a village called Centennial for more music and food; along with meeting up with even more friends of my future host. From the rooftop of the bar in Centennial, I could see on one side the Rocky Mountains and the sun slowly setting behind them. On the other side the Great Plains with grass blowing in the wind like waves on an ocean.

After a few hours of drinking and listening to music in Centennial, we headed back to Laramie where we met even more people for a big game of kickball in the park before watching the fireworks over the town that night. The whole day was one mini-adventure after another- as one might expect from an excursion into what used to be the Wild West. From the festival, to the village in the hills, and the kickball in the park; *America Has a Birthday* was one of the best Fourth of July celebrations I never knew existed and was hands down one of the best, unexpected moments of any of my field studies.

"Your Side of Town" Maddie & Tae
The number three slot goes to an entire town's experience. While conducting my study on the history and role of women in rodeo, I often found my plans falling by the wayside when unexpected obstacles arose. One of those obstacles was my inability to find a third host in Laramie- where I had planned to stay before heading to Cheyenne to attend the major rodeo there. In response, I boarded a bus and went south to Fort Collins, Colorado where I was planning on using it as a base of operations while looking for a host during my scheduled time in Cheyenne.

In Laramie, I met a girl returning from a long rock climbing trip across Wyoming on her way back to Colorado. Along the bus ride, I tried to sleep-as I had not been getting very much during my time in Laramie. When I arrived in Fort Collins, the bus dropped me and two cowboys off on the outskirts of town- because apparently the city's bus stop is not inside the city.

After calling my Couchsurfer host to let her know where I was, I spoke with the two cowboys who were waiting for their rides. One was excited to learn I was an anthropologist and immediately began talking to me about Native American history and archaeology-especially after I told him about my archaeology dig at Kincaid Mounds. The other was excited to talk about Alaska when I told him I had been living in Sitka for the last two years- since he often fished in summers out of Ketchikan.

Alas, both cowboys hailed their rides before my host arrived to pick me up, so I spent the last few minutes listening to music while I waited for my ride. When my host arrived, I jumped in her car and she drove me back to her apartment. Along the way, she said she was eager to host me because she had a professor while attending the University of Nebraska who specialized in studying women in rodeo. When we got to Nebraska's apartment, she handed me a copy of her professor's book- trading it for my copy of *Siddhartha*. Nebraska was a piano teacher and she had a student on their way for a lesson, so she handed me a key to the subdivision pool and told me to go hand out in the water while she did her lesson.

The pool was an oasis after a long series of road trips- first from Saint Louis to Laramie and then Laramie to Fort Collins- made even better by the presence of a hot tub. After sufficiently enjoying the watering hole solo, I headed back into my host's apartment where her lesson had ended. After taking a quick shower, Nebraska drove me out to a local bar which was hosting an open mic night. It also unknowingly hosted a Couchsurfer party.

Apparently, Fort Collins has a strong Couchsurfer community, so when Nebraska told her friends she was taking me out to a bar, seven other Couchsurfing members showed up. Over the course of the evening, the nine of us talked about the website and about world travels. We talked about music and sports, and spent the evening drinking and socializing. Inside, women sand sea shanties as the open mic night died down, and I started playing pool with a woman from Anchorage. (Alaskans are everywhere!)

When Nebraska's boyfriend arrived, the three of us headed to get some late-night food and headed back to her apartment to share an after-party meal. The next day, I met up with one of the other people from the unintentional Couchsurfing party who was interested in learning more about fencing. I met up with the graphic design artist from Ohio at the university where I taught him footwork and warm-up drills I use in fencing. After our fencing lesson, he took me out to one of his favorite restaurants- a Dungeons and Dragons themed bar with countless board games and themed menu items.

After lunch, Cleveland dropped me off at Nebraska's apartment. I headed back to the pool while my host taught another piano lesson and ended up talking to an architecture student about Neri Oxman (which, if you don't know who she is; look her up). After the pool visit, I headed back inside Nebraska's apartment and got ready for another night out. She threw me a motorcycle helmet and asked if I wanted to ride on the back of her bike to the bar.

"Let's do it!" I exclaimed as I strapped the helmet on and hopped on the bike. (Admittedly, it was a moped- but, come on.)

I held on to the bike as she drove us to the bar to see a comedy night with a couple of her roommates. The fun part was that the attendance (including myself) were the judges- which meant we got to decide who won the prize for that night. After a few decent acts, one man got on stage as the last comedian and made jokes about public transit and online dating and absolutely killed it.

The next day, Nebraska was preparing for a trip of her own to South Dakota where her adoptive brother was having a ceremony with his Native Community (I want to say Lakota, but I could be wrong) to become an official adult in his tribe. After my brief goodbye salute to the oasis of a pool, Nebraska drove me to Cleveland's apartment as he would be hosting me for the next couple nights.

At the time Cleveland was hosting another Couchsurfer who was in town for a religious conference (Judaism) at the university. Cleveland took me to a bar to meet up with a friend of his who he met while in the Air Force in Wyoming. Cleveland's friend had become a contract photographer and would be going to the rodeo in Cheyenne to photograph the event.

After dinner, Cleveland and I went back to his place to play board games with the other Couchsurfer who had returned from her meetings for the day. The next day, I had coffee with Cleveland at his apartment before heading to a nearby coffee shop to use their internet and to charge my electronics. That night, Cleveland took me to an underground jazz bar where we met two women in town on vacation- one who had a nine-year old daughter who competed in barrel racing.

Cleveland then took me to another bar to play bar games (Cornhole). After I soundly defeated him three times in a row, he bought me a beer and we talked about the stark differences between Wyoming and Colorado cultures. The next day, I spent the afternoon watching *Batman: The Animated Series* with Cleveland before he drove me to my final Fort Collins Couchsurfer host- a young woman who worked with a taco truck in town.

Fort Collins was not actually on Couchsurfing, but her friend was. Since her friend couldn't host me (since she was out of town), but was also impressed by my being a feminist anthropologist- her friend (Fort Collins) was eager to host me. On the first night, Fort Collins tested my knowledge of matrilinialism [feminine defined descent] and matritheology [women's studies and religious studies intertwined]. The next morning, she handed me several books to eagerly learn how many of them I had read before she left for work. While Fort Collins was at work, I read the several books I had not read before my host's introduction. When she came back, we shared dinner and coffee before watching *Scooby Doo* on my computer.

While staying with Cleveland, I decided not to go to Cheyenne and instead save the little money I had left to take a bus to Seattle early. After staying with Fort Collins for two nights, I hopped on a bus and left the city of Fort Collins behind me to continue my adventure across the American West. During my time there, I met some incredibly generous people, judged comedians, had lunch next to a group of Furies [people who dress like animals], and rode on the back of a cute girl's motorcycle. As far as unplanned stops go, Fort Collins was pretty good.

"Unstoppable" Lianne La Havas

The number two best unplanned moment goes to an evening that involved mega-chess, soaking my feet in a Calvinist monument, doing zumba by a river, talking poetry with a physicist, and watching an outdoor movie. This spot goes to my impromptu day trip to Geneva. During my fencing study in Europe, I went to a lot of towns more out of a "why not" philosophy" than out of a "why" philosophy. Apart from Milan (where my flights arrived in and departed from) and Leipzig (where the target tournament would be) I mostly just pulled out a map and thought, "Fuck it, let's go there!"

One of these towns was Geneva, Switzerland. I've had a lot of friends who have been to Europe and they all told me Switzerland was too expensive for them to get to- meaning if I went, I'd be the only one in my circle of friends who had been to Switzerland. (So you better believe this arrogant prick bought a train ticket to Switzerland.) I chose a hostel outside of Geneva since it was the cheapest hostel in the whole country. After sleeping my first night there, I spent the morning doing laundry in the hostel laundry room.

It was there that I met a young man from Sweden who was on his first trip outside of Scandinavia and who was also a member of the Couchsurfing website. He told me he was going to meet up with some folks in downtown Geneva and invited me to come along. I made sure to inform Sweden on my sadistic sense of humor before relentlessly joking about how he was one ear away from looking like Vincent Van Gogh.

When Sweden and I got to Geneva, we met with a local Couchsurfer who took us to a park which housed several sets of meter-tall chess pieces. Geneva and Sweden challenged me to a game (which I of course won) before we got ice cream nearby. Geneva told us while we ate out ice cream another group of Couchsurfing members- this time from Italy- were en route, so she took us to a Calvinist fountain where we dipped our feet in while waiting for the other people. When they arrived, we talked for an hour before they left to get dinner. Geneva, Sweden, and I grabbed street food before rushing to another park to catch an outdoor movie.

There, Geneva introduced us to a different group of Couchsurfers on a meet-up who were picnicking before the designated movie start time. The three of us gladly accepted the food offers from the group which included people from Lebanon, Germany, Italy, and Switzerland- and food that included wine, bread, cookies, beer, pretzels, and cheese. I want to state here that none of the cheese had holes in it. I kept asking if it was from Italy, France, or Germany because I refused to believe cheese without holes could come from Switzerland. (This is bullshit, and is why this did not get the number one spot.)

Before the movie began, the projector displayed a *Dance Dance Revolution* zumba- which I rocked- before hyping the crown up with *Queen* music. (To which everybody sang.) The film was a movie about a LGBT group in 1970's England raising money for Welsh coal miners on strike. In a scene during the film, a spokesman for the miners was invited to speak at a gay bar the night he first met the LGBT group. He told the patrons of the bar that there was no greater feeling in the world than meeting a friend you never knew you had- a quote that sticks with me today.

In Geneva, I had met such incredible people and ate such incredible food (excluding the hole-less cheese because that's bullshit). On the train ride back to the hostel, Sweden and I teased each other. I was impressed by Sweden's adaption to my style of humor. He didn't have a lot of money and we were running late to catch the train. so I told him we could just board the train without paying.

"What?" Sweden asked nervously. "What if the police ask for our tickets?"

"Do you still have your ticket from this morning?" I asked.

"Yes," Sweden replied. "But it's only one way!"

"Well, so is mine," I returned.

"So what will we do?" he reiterated.

"Oh, I'll just blame you," I returned jokingly.

"Yeah, fuck you!" Sweden spoke as he boarded the train with me.

During the train ride, a policeman walked past us. I gave Sweden this look that said, "keep it cool man," as the man walked past. He never asked us for tickets and we got off at our stop. The two of us laughed for the entire walk back to the hostel. (There were also several "fuck you"s thrown around. Good times.) By the way, any world travelers reading this: go ahead and don't do what I did. There are actually pretty hefty fines in Europe- and especially Switzerland- for riding public transit without a ticket.

"California Friends" The Regrettes

The number one greatest unplanned moment of any of my first four years of writing about women's sports is a no-contest moment where I got to not only meet some of my favorite athletes spontaneously, but painted beside them. The greatest unplanned moment goes to my painting session with the Seattle Reign- my favorite soccer team. While recovering in Seattle after almost two months worth of road trips during my study on the role and history of women in rodeo, I had to regularly go to the bank each morning to pull out money because I lost my debit card in Colorado. While in the bank one day, a teller recognized my Wonder Woman coffee mug and proudly displayed her Wonder Woman lego figure at her desk.

While talking about Wonder Woman and about my research, a woman in the next line overheard us talking. "Do you follow women's soccer at all?" she asked me without noticing the Seattle Reign jersey I was wearing.

"I do," I spoke with a chuckle. "I actually wrote my first book about women's soccer.

"Well," she replied, "I work for the hospital across the street and in half an hour, some of the women who play for Seattle's women's team will be coming to help paint some murals for the cancer ward. You should come by and meet them."

I had one of those moments where instinct kicked in. Sometimes, I am thrust into a position where if I allowed myself to be fully aware of my actions, it might impede my ability to handle the situation, so I respond to surrendering to instinct. This was one of those moments. Someone had just invited me to meet members of my favorite soccer team- professional athletes, athletes whose jerseys I have hanging up on my wall- as a casual offer.

"Yeah," I replied without pause. "I will definitely be there."

The woman gave me directions to where to go before leaving the bank. After finishing pulling money out, I grabbed a quick lunch to try to suppress any excitement from my body before heading to the hospital. Inside, I sat at a table where a six foot by three foot paint-by-number rested and two hospital staff members greeted me. The woman who recommended my presence introduced me to the staff and I began painting.

Only a couple minutes later, members of the Seattle Reign arrived. I was starting to freak out, but I kept my cool. That was until Beverly Yanez and Nahomi Kawasumi sat down next to me and started painting with me. (Beverly fucking Yanez!!!) I spent the next two hours with the two athletes as we painted the piece on the table (a parrot if I remember correctly). We talked about my research and about Japan's women's league. (Both had played in Japan before coming to the NWSL in 2014). Both athletes were impressed that I knew about that.

When our painting was done, the two let me get a photo with them before I left. As soon as I walked out of the hospital, all of the emotions I managed to suppress for the last two hours hit me all at once and I started dancing on the sidewalk, fist-bumping the air, and jumping ecstatically- and of course posting that picture with the two athletes all over social media. I then turned around and the team was right behind me.

"Hi again!" I spoke nervously.

Yanez laughed, "Hi again!" she spoke before walking off with the team.

"Shining Star" Nneka

Every once in a while, I count myself lucky when experiencing a particular moment. For example, I live in Sitka, Alaska- and if a person reading this has never been to where I live, they should know that the town is located on an island and is sandwiched between the mountains and the ocean. Since there are few people here and even fewer large barges floating around, whales will often come close to shore- and on an almost daily basis in October, I will see dozens of whales at a time breach from just about any building's window in the town. (To the point that I often take this for granted.)

But "mega-events" (like seeing a pod of whales breaching and feeding) are not the only moments that can inspire awe. Sometimes, I see small, "micro-events" like watching a celebrity take the time to talk to their fans (like that famous photo of Gal Gadot and the little girl dressed as Wonder Woman). I'm lucky enough to have seen both incredible moments of awe inspired by acts of both nature (like sunsets or sunrises) and kindness (like athletes signing autographs for little girls.)

The number five spot actually goes to a combination of micro-events all related to the Leipzig World Championships that were both awe-inspiring *and* awe-inducing. Throughout the event, I got to speak with a wide and diverse range of fans at the tournament to cheer on their respective favorite teams and athletes fencing in the world championships. During a break between bouts, Russian fencer Yana Egorian was sitting in the stands and checking in on social media on her phone. When she looked up from her phone, a nervous six-year-old girl was standing nervously in front of her with a t-shirt from the tournament and a Sharpie.

"Aww!" Egorian spoke before continuing in what I want to assume was Russian for "Would you like me to sign that?"

The girl nodded and handed over the shirt to the athlete in front of her and Egorian signed the girl's shirt. The little girl then grabbed the shirt and ran off more excited than I think I have ever been and met who I assume was her mom away from the bleachers. As big of a smile that little girl had while carrying off her autographed shirt, I recall seeing an equally big smile on Egorian's face as she collected her things and returned to the competition floor.

A couple days later, I was sitting between bouts in the seating overlooking the athlete warm-up area. One of the young volunteers at the tournament was sitting with her mom watching the athletes warm up. After striking up a conversation with the two, I found out the girl had just started taking fencing lessons and had thus far been contemplating whether or not she wanted to keep doing it. After she left to go back to work, her mom told me that after watching some of the women at the tournament compete, her daughter became excited to keep doing fencing because of how inspired she was by the athletes she watched- learning how badass women in sports can be, especially women in fencing.

A similar situation arose on the last day of competition. While I watched the US women's epee team compete against China, a mom and her two young children (a boy aged five and a girl aged six) sat down next to me. The family were all Germans who came to watch the tournament. The mom was hoping having her kids watch the athletes might inspire one of them to want to try fencing. (As I learned early in my study, there are only ever two sports that kids in Germany ever join- soccer or fencing.)

The boy was running all over the place and wanting to go home- to which I joked "I think he's going to do soccer."

The little girl however was standing in awe while watching the American and Chinese women compete. I talked to her mom about the four athletes that made up the American team (Anna Van Brummen, Kat Holmes, and Kelly and Courtney Hurley). I think a lot of sports writers often get to watch an athlete or a team win a gold medal- whether at a championship event or an Olympic Games (and that is its own awe-inspiring moment), but few people are lucky enough to see the moment when a little girl has that one moment- that superhero origin story. I knew as soon as I saw that little girl in awe while watching the American women that she would become a world-class fencer one day.

"Big Smoke" Tash Sultana
The number four spot for most awe-inspiring moments goes to an act of nature. I grew up going camping once a month until I graduated high school, so I've seen a lot of mountains, deserts, lakes,

and islands in my day. One of the things that kept me from leaving the United States was the belief that anything the rest of the world has (mountains, deserts, etc) the US also has- so I could just see the American version. For the most part I was still correct. The Gulf of Mexico from Pensacola, Florida looked almost exactly like the Mediterranean from Bogliasco, Italy and the Black Forest in Bavaria looked almost exactly like the Ozarks in Southern Missouri. One feature of European geography however stood apart from anything I had ever seen though- the Swiss Alps.

While taking the bus from Munich to Milan during my field study on the role of women in fencing, the bus drove up and down the mountainous tops of the Austrian and Swiss Alps. Along the ride, I could see from my window flocks of sheep roaming across the grass of the mountains, little lakes dotting the valleys between peaks, shepherds and their dogs herding dairy cows, and some of the most magnificent waterfalls overlooking towns which consist of homes probably built in the Medieval times.

The bus stopped several times to fill up with gas or pick-up and drop off passengers, but one of the stops was in Zurich and it was incredible. The bus driver let us know it would take about half an hour to refill the bus with gas so we were welcome to walk inside the terminal. I stayed outside under the open-air ceiling of the bus terminal though to take pictures of the scene around me. There were several dozen-story buildings and between the architecture was the massive expanse of the Swiss Alps. Everything fell under a sunny, blue sky and I felt like I was breathing the freshest air in the world. (I was legitimately waiting for some Disney-style cartoon birds to land on my shoulders and start singing.)

"Heat" Leyya

What is probably the winner of the number one coolest moment I have ever had get the spot for third most awe-inspiring moments. During my study on the role of women in surfing, a lot of incredible and unplanned moments happened, from defeating a Costa Rican in a dance-off to swimming under the night sky in Hawaii. Perhaps the most awe-inspiring moment of my surf study though came when I won a raffle prize in the form of a world champion surfer's personal surfboard.

While at the beach one day with a group of fellow hostellers, we noticed one of the tournament competitors practicing in the water during what was a "lay day" [meaning the competition was called off]. Adelaide (the one of us from the group of four from Australia) realized the surfer was Nikki Van Dijk- one of his favorite athletes- so when we noticed her heading back to the beach, we headed over to go meet her.

Adelaide and Nikki spoke for a few moments, and I took pictures for them. Nikki then told us about an autographing event at one of the Rip Curl outlets near the hostel and told us we should go. There would be several professional surfers there with door prizes and raffle give-aways to support charities. Adelaide left that night, so he wasn't able to go, but I went to the event with several other hostellers.

There were several prizes- including water bottles, t-shirts, and even wetsuits- but the top prize for the raffle was a surfboard used by world champion Tyler Wright, painted on by top surf painter Drew Brophy, and autographed by several professional surfers. Throughout the event, the announcer handed several prizes off to some of the guests at the hostel while everyone eagerly awaited the announcement for who would win the surfboard. Finally, the announcer read the ticket number for the surfboard and I felt the biggest smile I ever had on my face. I casually strolled up to the announcer and showed my ticket.

"I believe that's my board," I spoke confidently.

The announcer looked at my ticket and smiled, "That *is* your board!"

The officials handed me Tyler's surfboard and a representative came over with a microphone to ask me questions like, "What's your name?" and "Where are you from?" before allowing the other hostellers to rush me in congratulations. We strolled into a liquor store en route to the hostel and stocked up for the celebration ahead. At the hostel, the staff took pictures with all of us winners with our prizes.

In surfing lingo, there's a term for unfiltered joy called "frothin" and I was the textbook definition of the term that day. I tossed around beers and celebrated with everyone at the hostel. When I finally got back home to Sitka a couple weeks later, I set up the board in full display to remind me of that moment every morning when I wake up. (By the way, if under some miracle that Tyler Wright is reading this; you are always welcome to come visit your surfboard in Sitka, Alaska. That would give me serious cred in my town.)

"Sun to Sun" Kaia Kater

The second most awe-inspiring moment I experienced during my field studies came with a double-overlay of history. While conducting my study on the role of women in rodeo, I quickly learned I would need to experience the history of the American West. My plan then was to roughly follow the Oregon Trail from St. Louis, Missouri to the Pacific Ocean. During the original treks across the route, migrants would have to cross swamps, deserts, mountains, and plains; would have to deal with hunger, illness, wild animals; and would only survive on their will to keep going, kindness from Native Peoples, and the belief that a better life awaited them on the other side.

During my rodeo study, my journey mirrored the Oregon Trail more than I would have liked. I ran dangerously low on funds (especially when I lost my debit card), relied on the kindness of modern natives (Couchsurfer hosts), and had to overcome the obstacles of distance yet-to-travel, mountains yet-to-cross, and a friend that prematurely departed along the way. On the bus ride from Denver to Oregon, I felt my will breaking; believing that nothing could salvage my study and that I had failed.

When the bus reached a small town outside of Pendleton, Oregon at one in the morning, the driver dropped us off in the parking lot of a McDonald's where the next bus would pick us up. The problem was that the bus would not be picking the ten of us passengers up until seven am. There were no hotels, motels, or even Couchsurfer hosts in the village where we found ourselves; so we took turns with sentinel duty while the rest of us slept in shifts under the night sky in the McDonald's parking lot.

In the early morning, I woke up and looked East toward the Rocky Mountains where the early rays of sun announced the day's arrival. While watching the sun rise over the mountains, I felt something I had never felt before. The sun warmed my face and there was a sense of hope and accomplishment- that I not only did not fail, but that I accomplished everything I had set out to do. I made it. I crossed swamps, plains, deserts, and mountains; and soon, I would see the Pacific Ocean.

I understood in that moment everything everyone who had successfully journeyed the Oregon Trail felt when they did the same I had done. (I even teared up a little.) I knew in that moment, that I could survive anything- that no matter how difficult an obstacle, I could overcome it. When the bus came shortly after to pick us up, I left my sense of broken will behind in that village in Eastern Oregon and entered Seattle later that day with renewed strength which I still carry with me today.

"The Wire" HAIM

The number one most awe-inspiring moment wins the top spot because it was unlike any other. When I was in Germany for the Leipzig World Championships, I got to witness a little girl's "superhero origin" moment where I saw her mesmerized by the women competing in front of her. The number one spot for this list goes to my own "superhero origin" moment- the moment where I realized what I wanted to do with my life; the moment where I was exactly where I was supposed to be and doing exactly what I was supposed to be doing with my life- and that moment happened while I was in Canada for the 2015 FIFA Women's World Cup.

I stayed in Vancouver for three weeks while watching the games of the FIFA Women's World Cup. I went because I realized the previous summer that Vancouver would be the closest world cup to Alaska there would probably ever be. I never intended on writing a book, on interviewing athletes, or making friends along the way; but somehow I managed to do all of those things.

While in Canada, I felt a sense of foresight as each day brought me closer to something I could feel would be life changing. When the final game arrived on July 5th, I went to go watch Japan and the United States square off in the final game. There were wildfires in nearby Vancouver Island that summoned thick smoke in Vancouver which made the entire city smell like a bonfire. During the game, I never sat down because the two teams were constantly scoring goal-after-goal, making impressive plays, and urging the crowd on as they fought on the pitch.

When the game ended, the United States won the match and the tournament. Confetti exploded everywhere, emotional music played, and the US team collected their trophy. From the moment the game began to the moment the first American athlete touched the trophy, I felt like time had suspended. After the award ceremony ended however, I felt like it all sped up twice as fast to make up for the slow motion and in a moment; it seemed like I was the last person standing in the stadium.

I quickly realized how special of a moment I witnessed was; and said goodbye to the stadium before wiping the tears from my face and leaving the building. After partying in downtown Vancouver at one of the bars with several other fans, I finally headed back to the hostel in Jericho Beach. Sleep was impossible- even late in the night, so when I heard a familiar voice coming from outside my dorm window, I headed outside to find Montpellier (one of the friends I made along that crazy journey) who also could not sleep.

Montpellier and I walked to the beach and talked about what we saw that day, about how inspiring it all was, and about what it would mean for the future of women's sports. I remember looking out across the water toward downtown Vancouver with the thick smoke of the wildfires still falling on the city. On that beach on that night, a voice appeared in the back of my mind telling me that I was where I was supposed to be, doing what I was supposed to be doing- so when I headed home the next day, I began writing the book that would become *Behind the Goal*.

I think very few people are lucky enough to have a moment like what I had on my last night in Vancouver. To be completely overwhelmed with the feeling that I had found what it was in life I was meant to do is probably the most important moment of my life. It inspired me to go further and to challenge me to explore more sports and explore more corners of the world than I had ever explored. (Plus I got to spend the evening on a beach with a beautiful French woman, so…)

Epilogue

"Out Here" Kiah Victoria

Returning home from a life-changing adventure is never easy. Whether a person returns from backpacking across Europe, hitchhiking across the American West, or island-hopping across the Pacific; returning to the solace of everyday life at home can be its own kind of culture shock. Luckily, I was at least a little bit familiar with this feeling. As a child, I was in a lot of sports, Boy Scouts, and several after-school activities. When a sports season would end (say track & field) there was a sense of emptiness that came with no longer having practices to attend after school.

But when my adventures became longer than one week, I started feeling like I was wasting my days. When I returned home from Canada after the women's world cup, I had spent so much time in a hostel where I could wake up in the morning and have people to talk to and got get lunch with or coffee or whatever; that when I got home and woke up in the morning to have no one to have breakfast with, I went crazy.

When I returned home from any trip after that that involved a hostel, I had locked my mind into a habit of waking up, having breakfast with people I never met before, going somewhere with new friends, and celebrating the privilege of traveling together. The problem then was when I returned home, I found people perfectly content with not meeting new people. Meeting new people while in my own town was impossible. Nobody cared that I wrote about women's sports. Nobody cared that I lived in Alaska (though to be fair, we all lived in Alaska.) And most importantly, nobody wanted to meet new people. Everyone was perfectly content with their social bubble.

I don't like those kinds of people. Even in my own town; I enjoy meeting new people, listening to points-of-view that challenge and counter my own, exploring music I've never heard before, eating food I've never tasted before, and most importantly- just talking to people over coffee. So, frustrated with the lack of having any of this in my own town; within weeks of finishing one book I always begin planning for the next.

For anyone reading this either before or after an adventure of their own, worried about re-acclimating to life after an adventure; don't. Life changing adventures should challenge you to see the world through new perspectives- so don't let the familiarity of home lure you back into being who you used to be. And if everyone around you seems to be comfortable in their lack of meeting new people, don't let that personality trait convert you from wanting to meet new people and try new things. Go try a new restaurant or a new coffee shop. Find a person at a friend's party you've never met and say hi. Adventures don't always have to start half-way around the world- in fact, some of the greatest adventures happen when you begin to explore your own backyard. And from there, there's no knowing where you might go.

"What I'll Do" Lisa Hannigan

While re-acclimating to home after an adventure can be difficult, perhaps more difficult is knowing what to do with your experiences. Especially as an anthropologist, I struggled early on with taking notes on my experiences and putting them into words. While anyone is certainly welcome to take this section as advice, I'd like to dedicate it specifically to any budding young anthropologists reading who may need help with knowing what (and whatnot) to put in their field journals.

Luckily, my first field study came while I was still in college; so by the time I got to Canada for my study on the role of women in international soccer, I already had an idea of how to take notes. Keeping a field journal is essential for a number of reasons, but most important is that human memory is a tricky thing. I personally have notoriously terrible memory, so I keep a field journal with extremely detailed notes so that I won't have to rely on memory while writing a book.

Sometimes the problem with learning anthropology in the classroom of a university can be difficult too because some socio-cultural anthropologists conduct studies that require a certain amount of censorship, questionably legal activity, or sensitive information about individuals. For example, Margaret Mead traveled to Samoa in the mid Twentieth Century to take notes on the sexual activity of teenage girls. That's really not something people should be able to know who exactly did what or with whom. Or an anthropologist studying the drug trade and how it affects addicts on the street definitely does not want their study to lead to people getting arrested or the anthropologist themselves getting killed.

With those examples, the best first thing to know about a field journal is anonymity. I never write persons' names in my field journals- instead coming up with a code system for names (replacing names with cities, countries, or states). Plus, this makes for good nicknames around the hostel. Anyone reading the book will have no clue who a person is unless I want them to know (such as a professional athlete).

To go back to Margaret Mead, the famous anthropologist once quoted that "What a person says, what a person does, and what a person says they do are all completely different things."

The problem with interviewing people can be that if they know you're going to be writing about the conversation you're having, that knowledge can make them say things they might think you want to hear or make them say things they might not want people to know they said. There is definitely a gray area for ethics here. At one end, you want people to know what they say might end up in a book, but on the other end if you tell that to someone, they might not answer questions truthfully and your interview is useless.

My middle ground here is that I will only ever touch my field journal in the morning when I wake up or at night before I go to bed. I let people know I write about women's sports so they have an idea of why I'm in town, but they don't know I might write about the conversation we have. When I have a conversation with someone extremely sexist who does not realize I'm going to add everything I say to the book I'm writing, I'll feel bad for a moment and then remind myself, "Fuck that guy, if he doesn't want this conversation to go public, he shouldn't be such a sexist asshole." And then I write it down.

The other aspect that I highly suggest about field journals is they should be in an actual journal. I tried writing field journals on a computer, but for a number of reasons, having a physical notebook- especially a small, pocket sized one- will always beat electronic technology. For one, I can carry that journal easily in my pocket and a pen or pencil also fits nicely into the same pocket.

Also, there's a sense of adventure that comes with scribbling into a notebook that I never felt tapping my fingers on a keyboard.

(This might come from years of camping once a month.) And
ultimately, if my computer crashes, I will lose all of my field notes;
but if I keep them written on paper, I can grab that notebook off of
my shelf at home and reminisce about adventures passed and feel all
the emotions return as my fingers touch the dried ink and rough
pages stained with coffee rings and dirt.

"Postureo" Beatriz Luengo

When I've written all there is to write, publish a book, and
see my work on one study complete; I never hesitate before planning
another. This can be difficult though. Especially with a topic like
women's sports, the obstacle of picking a new topic to write about is
like looking at a buffet and picking where to start. Most of the time, I
end a study with more questions than I had at the start as well. In the
case of soccer, I wanted to know most importantly what sport was
the first to give women pay equal to their male counterparts. As was
the case with fencing where athletes are covered from head to toe, I
wanted to know about a sport where athletes wear almost nothing.

But knowing where to go next is just like knowing where to
go at any point along an adventure- whether at the start of
somewhere in the middle- at all boils down to "why not?" instead of
"why?". The thing with writing a book is that writing is the easy
part. People sometimes struggle with this concept- but it goes
beyond writing. Painting or singing or any form of art is actually
extremely easy. The difficult part is making something people
actually care about. To make something people care about, the artist
must be the first person to care. If a person writes a book about a
topic they personally don't care about, nobody will care. So when I
write about the sports I write about, my first question is which sport
I've always wanted to learn more about.

Before I began writing about women's sports, I actually
joked one time with an old friend that the only sport I ever really
watched was women's tennis. Now, I have the schedules for soccer,
rodeo, surfing, fencing, basketball, and tennis all scribbled into my
calendar. I watch every event I can during both the Winter and
Summer Olympics, follow athletes across sports from figure skating
and skiing to swimming and rock climbing. At the time I wrote *this*

book, I had the jerseys of ten athletes from four sports decking the walls of my apartment.

I don't know what books I will write in the future; what adventures await me. Maybe I'll play Scrabble with members of USA Swimming or I'll find myself drinking Guinness with camogie players in Ireland. But whatever adventures await- however more I have left in me- I'm reminded of a story about two pirates I added to the book I wrote about women in fencing.

An older pirate who retired from the seas and came back for one last adventure tells the young captain of the ship to keep going for as long as he can. Traveling and writing my books is expensive and I really do not sell enough books to even break even, let alone profit from, these studies. But each adventure challenges me to see the world from new points of view and to find parts of myself I never knew existed.

Doctor Seuss once wrote that "Unless someone cares a whole awful lot, nothing will ever change, it will not." So for as long as I am passionate about what I write about (women actually having human rights) I will keep going- just like the pirate in the story. And, if anyone reading this has something they care "a whole awful lot" about, do everything you can and go as far as you can. The world needs more people like that. (Unless you like killing people. We don't need more of that.)

In the rare event that any anthropologist, potential sponsor, badass athlete, or family member who's forgotten my contact information interested in getting in contact with me; please do! I would love to talk women's sports, feminist anthropology, Wonder Woman comics, favorite flavors of ice cream, etc with all of you! Please send an email to josephwilsonanthro@gmail.com.

"Different." Ximena Sarinana. *Ximena Sarinana*; Warner Records Inc. 2011.

"Keep Diggin'." Larkin Poe. *Keep Diggin'*; Tricki-Woo Records. 2020.

"Out On The Roan." Norah Jones. *Little Broken Heart*; Blue Note Records. 2012.

"Boom Fire." HIRIE. *Wandering Soul*; Hirie Music. 2016.

"Hot to the Touch." Grace Potter. *Midnight*; Hollywood Records. 2015.

"Mixer." Amber Mark. *Mixer*; PMR Records. 2019.

"Abduction." Simonne Jones. *Abduction*; Simonne Jones. 2020.

"Too Young to Remember." Florrie. *Too Young to Remember*; Sony Music Entertainment. 2015.

"Sunday." Anuhea. *For Love*; AnuheaJams. 2012.

"This Town." Kacey Musgraves. *Pageant Material*; Mercury Records. 2015.

"Your Side of Town." Maddie & Tae. *Start Here*; Republic Records. 2015.

"Unstoppable." Lianne La Havas. *Blood*; Warner Music UK. 2015.

"California Friends." The Regrettes. *How Do You Love*; Warner Records Inc. 2019.

"Heartbeat." Nneka. *No Longer At Ease*; Yo Mama's Recording Company. 2008.

"Big Smoke." Tash Sultana. *Flow State*; Lonely Lands Records. 2018.

"Heat." Leyya. *Suana*; +1 Records. 2018.

"Sun to Sun." Kaia Kater. *Sorrow Bound*; Kingswood Records. 2015.

"The Wire." HAIM. *Days Are Gone*; Columbia Records. 2012.

"Out Here." Kiah Victoria. *Memo EP*; Tralala Records. 2010.

"What I'll Do." Lisa Hannigan. *Passenger*; ATO Records. 2011.

"Postureo." Beatriz Luengo. *Cuerpo y Alma*; Sony Music Entertainment. 2018

www.ingramcontent.com/pod-product-compliance
Lightning Source LLC
Chambersburg PA
CBHW051401250726
48656CB00006B/2205